Becoming a
HECKUVACHIC®
(heck•of•a•chick)

How to Become a **Heckuvachic** after Experiencing Life's Disappointing Setbacks

Kristie S. Andrews, MBA, FACHE, CPXP, CPC, CDP®

For information regarding special discounts for bulk purchases, please contact the publisher: LaBoo Publishing Enterprise, LLC
staff@laboopublishing.com
www.laboopublishing.com

Illustrator: Jada Abney
Photographer: Alvin Hinton Photography
Makeup: J'Dior Artistry
Book Cover Design: Briative
Book Editing: Kirkus

FOREWORD

If you are searching for someone to help you crack the code to overcoming life's obstacles so that you live differently, then this book is a must-read. Kristie S. Andrews is a certified professional life coach, and she provides impactful tools in this book that can enhance your ideal life. She can guide you on your journey as she shares real-life situations and transformational insights that can help you along the way.

Kristie is well educated, experienced, and passionate about helping women become phenomenal. While using her tools, she is very mindful of your goals. This book is not designed to tell you what your goals are or should be. It is meant to broaden your horizons and help you seek that which is important to establish your foundation and accomplish your goals. She has a wide range of personal and professional experience that can help you change the trajectory of your life. If your goal is to climb the corporate ladder, she can coach you on how to go after your dream job. She will share secrets to her successful career and encourage you to do the same. If you need to gain clarity, confidence, purpose, drive, and ambition she can coach you on living your best life. Kristie provides a life-changing coaching experience for the woman on the go so she can become the Heckuvachic she's intended to be. If you are currently in a rut because of past personal relationships, this book can help you address those issues too.

Kristie has a certain way of approaching your issues with tact and diplomacy, which is an innate talent. Friends and family have always been able to approach her and receive sound advice for navigating personal problems and events. I am proud of her for finally realizing her talents and for her willingness to share her gift with women across the world. So, if you desire a breakthrough in your life, please break out of your shell and become the Heckuvachic that you are empowered to be.

—*Deborah Cherry, Kristie S. Andrews' mother*

CONTENTS

Foreword iii

Introduction:
Gaining Perspective on My Life Makeover. 1

Chapter 1: Woe Is Not Me? Excuse me, ma'am.
May I please interrupt your self-doubt? 15

Chapter 2: Becoming a Heckuvachic! 27

Chapter 3: Feel . . . the Emotion 35

Chapter 4: Forgive . . . Yourself and Others 43

Chapter 5: Free Your Mind . . .
from the Things That No Longer Serve You 53

Chapter 6: Find Your Voice . . . to Speak Your Truth 69

Chapter 7: Follow Your Dreams . . .
to Become the Heckuvachic You're Entitled to Be 81

Chapter 8: Turning Your Dreams into Plans! 89

Conclusion:
Let Your Self-Discovery Be Your Life's Breakthrough 95

INTRODUCTION:

Gaining Perspective on My Life Makeover

"Not all storms come to disrupt your life,
some come to clear your path." —Unknown

INTRODUCTION:

Gaining Perspective on My Life Makeover

As I kissed my husband's lifeless face goodbye, I immediately felt my inner spirit, soul, and self-identity leave my physical body. My heart was shattered into a million pieces. My mind was foggy, and I couldn't rationalize anything or anyone. I felt betrayed by life. I questioned my faith. This was a fast blow to my gut that I would not wish on my worst enemy. I experienced a pain that burned like hell in the pit of my stomach and penetrated every corner of my being.

I became a widow at age thirty-nine. He was my middle school sweetheart, who later became my best friend, my true love, my husband, and a father to my children. How unfair is that? My kids were so young, and the youngest one really didn't quite understand what was happening. Their childhood innocence was yanked from them. I loved him hard. I lost so much. He and I were supposed to raise our kids together. I didn't sign up to be a single parent.

I often imagined him and what kind of father he would be when the girls became teenagers. He loved his girls. My late husband was our protector. Nothing in this world made him happier than being a father to his girls. My children deserved their father. He died a slow death, and I was furious. I found myself emotionally, physically, and mentally bankrupt because what I was feeling was excruciating pain. You never get over the death of anyone you love and care about. It's a mistake if anyone believes this.

The days ahead became more difficult, uncomfortable, and emotionally unbearable. I looked in the mirror one day, and I was trying to figure out who the woman was staring back at me. I could not find myself. Who am I? What have I become? How did I lose myself in this life I call mine? I saw the physical shell of my body, but I could not find *me* as the tears filled my eyes. I felt incredibly and constantly broken, small, forgettable, and insignificant.

Not only was I feeling unspeakable pain and heartache, but my mental state was also not healthy. Your mindset has a very significant impact on your choices, decisions, and behavior. I was not in the healthiest place mentally. I didn't feel whole, and I felt like I would never have the life that I wanted because of suffering this tragic loss.

I thought, *Hmm. I have had my share of ups and downs, but this is the ultimate painful valley in my life.* I was still grieving the loss of a miscarriage three years prior to my husband's death. Life became increasingly and painfully dismal. My daughter had a near-drowning experience five months later. My mother and children were involved in a car crash. My mother had a massive heart attack as a passenger in my car while I was driving.

At this point, my life did not really have any meaning or hope beyond my beautiful and innocent children. I felt insecure, I felt alone, and *no one understood this*. The support group that I became a part of was filled with seniors who had lost their husbands or wives and most of them were over sixty-five and from different backgrounds and circumstances. We all became close and keep in touch until this day, but I had not yet met a widow who was my age that was going through what I was going through as a young mom with small children.

I had bouts of envy and jealously when seeing married couples together. I wondered why I had to experience this loss when I am a "good" person. I love God. I questioned if it was bad karma that caught up with me. Was it my fault? Should I have done things differently or should I have gotten a second opinion sooner? Should I have known that he had cancer before he was diagnosed? All these questions were circling my head moment after moment. These thoughts tended to distract me, and it became increasingly difficult to cope or merely function from day to day. I felt numb inside. I really didn't care about anything but my girls. I noticed I felt angry when seeing fathers with their children, especially with daughters.

It just wasn't fair. What could I have possibly done to deserve this much despair? I didn't like having these feelings. Who was going to walk my girls down the aisle? Who would protect us? How was I going to financially afford the implications of his death?

I frowned upon people who were envious and jealous in my past life. In fact, it was one of my pet peeves. I always felt that whatever you want in life can be yours if you did your part to get what you wanted. Life didn't have room for envy or jealousy. However, I quickly learned that these feelings were something I couldn't control at the time.

I couldn't just pick up and find a father for my children. I couldn't just meet someone who was my middle school sweetheart who knew me like the back of his hand. I could not replace the love that I missed and that I longed for. You see, he and I grew up in the same neighborhood five doors down from each other. We rode the same school bus together. We rode our bikes and played basketball together in our neighborhood park. Our girls' godparents lived in the same neighborhood.

Why did my life have to turn out this way? Why was this happening to my kids, to me, my husband's family, to his friends? Why did we lose someone who meant so much to us? These are questions no one could answer for me. Before his diagnosis he was salutatorian of his graduating college class. He worked so hard and was getting ready to change the trajectory of his career which would have a major impact on our lives. None of us could have imagined that our lives would be forever changed in this way.

My late husband passed in 2016, and a few years after his passing, I began to ponder how the hell I survived this tragic and painful loss. I noticed that I began to try to live a somewhat normal life again. By that, I mean I wasn't still in the bed, still not wanting to engage, interact, or fellowship with anyone I didn't necessarily have to. I wasn't as angry as I had been, and I wasn't as irritable. I wasn't crying uncontrollably. I didn't have random outbursts of extreme sadness and rage because of my grief anymore.

I was finally sleeping through the night. When I think about those lonely sleepless nights my heart aches because I can still feel the remnants of this feeling of misery. I began to think differently. I chose to change my mindset so that my future didn't feel hopeless anymore. I was still hurting, but I noticed that I wasn't feeling like my life was over.

I realized that I was not in a place of total shutdown anymore. I preferred to be in total shutdown, and I wondered why I wasn't. Surprisingly, my life began to flourish. I decided to explore and discover how and why I was able to close life's gap that left me heartbroken and lost.

I didn't feel an acute feeling of being emotionally, spiritually, mentally, and physically bankrupt. I wanted very much to understand why I was able to thrive instead of merely surviving.

This life of mine has brought me great successes, triumphs, and unbelievable joy. I have had my share of loss, trauma, disappointment, heartache, and feelings of hopelessness.

My life has had moments when it fell short of what I thought I wanted or needed in life. At times I have felt entrapped by an inability to own my life and go after the life I was entitled to have.

Think about a woman in your family, your circle of friends, a coworker, or a celebrity who has overcome insurmountable life challenges. Let's take Jennifer Hudson, world-renowned American singer, for instance. She lost several relatives in only three days. She undoubtedly transformed her life and was inspired to hope after that tragic event.

Through this tragedy, she built a foundation in honor of a loved one. She continues to win awards year after year. Although grief is forever, her soul speaks peace. She appears to be fulfilled. That's it! It's about bouncing back. I strongly believe that women are born with a level of self-resiliency that surpasses all understanding.

My childhood best friend, who is also my children's god-mother, suffered a massive stroke alone in her home in 2010 at the age of thirty-three. She survived, completed physical therapy, and did the work necessary to regain her life. She went on to become a pediatrician, author, and a badass woman who is stronger now than ever.

I've been chronically emotionally abused, dismissed, rejected, overlooked, marginalized, and I have been riddled with self-hatred for many years. At times I thought that my feelings and emotions didn't matter because of the abuse that I unfortunately suffered. Can you relate?

We know that destruction, pain, chaos, confusion, and sadness can't last forever. Sometimes our trials are merely temporary, and sometimes they are not. When you fall, you can get back up stronger than ever before. Out of our pain and life's setbacks comes our strength as we cannot allow them to define our futures.

Have you lost who you are as a woman? Many of you have a feeling of being stuck in life, and you're seeking a fresh perspective. I've been there. I have been broken-down, lost, and silent. I lived my life on autopilot for so very long. I was very stuck in my life, which led to heightened insecurity, fear, self-doubt, anxiety, self-hatred, and self-criticism. I lacked clarity, focus, purpose, meaning, and confidence to see what was possible in my life.

We have all had some type of unfortunate life experience. I wrote this book to help you with your life's breakthrough transformation, to help you own your personal power, to encourage you to gain a more positive mindset, and to motivate you to go after the life you've always dreamed—all by enhancing your emotional intelligence. I want to pass on the wisdom I learned from my pain so that you can make your life better. I don't want my suffering to be in vain; I want to share my self-discovery with you.

Emotional intelligence is simply understanding the capability of being aware of your emotions and social skills, and how you express empathy to others. This impacts us in our personal and professional lives. Understanding how you show up in your womanhood will unleash a sense of calm and peace in your life.

That's why it's so imperative to understand emotional intelligence and how your feelings, mindset, and emotions drive your thoughts, choices, and decisions. Understanding your own emotional intelligence is a prerequisite to becoming the Heckuvachic you are entitled to be.

Life can be relentless at times. Metaphorically speaking, I sometimes think of our lives as cars going on a road trip. We are always going to have *roadblocks* that act as barriers to the lives we desire. These roadblocks are unwanted and delay our progress forward in life.

We also at times have *speed limits* that cause us to slow down in life. I equate these speed limits to the limiting beliefs we tell ourselves, thoughts we believe to be true but are often preventing us from growing in life. Sometimes we hit a *fork* in the road, and it forces us to make life-changing decisions. Unfortunately, we are also going to experience *U-turns* in life. These U-turns can keep us from propelling forward in life; however, at times they can be just what we need to get redirected in the most optimal direction.

I also believe that we experience *traffic jams* throughout our life's journey. These traffic jams are moments of being stuck in life. These are times when you're lacking clarity, you're unfocused, and you're hoping for purpose to get through these jams. These experiences are inevitable when you live long enough.

You quickly realize that during these times, you need to put on your armor so that you can rise to the unantici-pated battles of life. But what is that armor? The armor is the Life Makeover Transformation Model I have designed and developed. I created this model to help you withstand life's unfortunate storms and persevere as you overcome life's roadblocks. Then and only then can you become the Heckuvachic that you are entitled to be and begin living what people call "your best life."

In the coming chapters, we will go through a journey of transparent life lessons that I have experienced.

I share specifically how these lessons are applicable to each step in my Life Makeover Transformation Model, so I encourage you to read this book in chronological order. Additionally, you'll have an opportunity to go a little deeper and access my "becoming a Heckuvachic" gift for you. My hope is that you will be inspired to make the necessary life breakthrough that you're looking for.

I will cover some heavy topics, but I sprinkle in my sense of humor. It's my belief that laughter is healing to the soul. Take this ride with me so that you can live life differently. You can and deserve to have a new, overwhelming, mind-blowing sense of life gratification. Embracing my own Life Makeover Transformation Model has opened my eyes to what's possible in life for me, and because of this, I can see clearly now.

Do you have the desire to blossom into a butterfly, but you still have the mindset of a caterpillar? What is the blueprint of your life? Only *you* can write or rewrite it. If your life is not what you want, please, ladies, *change it*! Are you just a passenger on your life bus? I need you to be the driver. Are you at a place in your life where you are ready to get out of your own way? Are you stuck by your limiting thoughts? Does your self-doubt get in the way of you doing what's possible? Are you doing life, or is life doing you? Are you going through the motions of life and not proactively living your life? I can most certainly relate.

I want you to join me on a journey. I provide a fresh perspective on life and share my tragic losses, heartache, struggles, pain, life roadblocks, traffic jams, U-turns, speed bumps, and detours that undoubtedly made me into the Heckuvachic I am today. For many years, I didn't know who I was, what my purpose was, and who I wanted to become. I had no dreams. I had feelings of helplessness and hopelessness. I was broken and disappointed with life. There were times when I thought that living my life in mediocracy was acceptable. This is my why. I don't want anyone else to go through life like this.

It is my belief that you will find that my Life Makeover Transformation Model will help you transform your mindset so that you can become the Heckuvachic you've always wanted to be. I don't want you to miss out on the life you know you desire and deserve. *Becoming a Heckuvachic* will have a positive impact on your romantic relationship, social life, career, finances, health and wellness, spiritual well-being, and family life. You must understand who you are and how you show up in the world. The trajectory of your life is at stake.

Maybe you don't recognize that you have unconscious baggage that is preventing you from moving forward in your life. I call BS on the years of baggage you continue to carry as a modern-day bag lady. I am allergic to BS. It makes me sneeze. It doesn't do anything for me, and it doesn't do anything for you.

I invite you to become a quitter. There, I said it. I want you to quit making excuses. I want you to quit making yourself your last priority. I want you to quit living your life according to what your family, friends, and society impart to you. We will no longer allow our insecurities to affect or control the journey of our lives. News flash, girlfriend: it's really *all* about you. There is no expiration date on your aspirations or dreams.

CHAPTER 1

Woe Is *Not* Me? Excuse me, ma'am. May I please interrupt your self-doubt?

"You are braver than you believe, stronger than you seem,
and smarter than you think."
—Christopher Robin

CHAPTER 1

Woe Is *Not* Me? Excuse me, ma'am. May I please interrupt your self-doubt?

Life was a smooth ride until life began to launch curveballs your way. Sometimes our lives are just the way we want them and then life situations occur, and they stop us in our tracks. At times these curveballs hurt, and they hurt like hell. It feels like someone spraying you with a firehose as you lie peacefully asleep, dreaming about your favorite celebrity crush.

It's because of these curveballs that we sometimes get stuck in life because of them. Life has a way of waking you up. You never see these curveballs. They are invisible. These curveballs never provide any heads-up. The curveballs hide, and they inevitably appear when we are enjoying peace in our everyday lives.

What life challenges are you having that are self-imposed? What are you tolerating now that you know you shouldn't? Guess what; you made mistakes before. We all do. Last time I checked, we are human, and that leads us to our strength. We can't continue to make the same mistakes repeatedly and expect our lives to change organically. Life doesn't work that way. It's up to us to change our mindsets so that our way of thinking helps us excel in life.

If you continue in a negative headspace, you will continue to feel hopeless and helpless. Your relationships will continue to suffer. Your career could bottom out. More importantly, your dreams will go unrealized because you've not worked on yourself.

Life is about transitions. Life can, unfortunately, bring heartache, pain, or a loss. We must accept that life is not a straight and comfortable path. The road gets rocky. Sometimes it becomes unmanageable. We can't see the potholes, so we get flat tires. We obey the law and stop at the stop sign but others may not. We sometimes yield to the needs of others while we are steadily backing up traffic in our own heads.

In my opinion, everything that happens to us is supposed to happen. Until we gain the superpowers necessary to predict life on demand, we will experience life's roadblocks and setbacks. All these experiences help to build our identities and character.

According to Cleveland Clinic, you have seventy thousand thoughts per day in your head. What's your ratio of positive thoughts to negative thoughts? For instance, think about the last time you had a life U-turn or traffic jam. Did it break you? You survived it, right? You are still here to talk about it. You found a way to cope, understand, and break through these setbacks. It's life. Unfortunately, we are not in control of setbacks that occur in our lives. We also must take personal accountability for our own thoughts, feelings, and actions. Sometimes it's difficult to learn these things after you've been the same way for so long. However, it can be done.

Who's been popping your bubble lately? Really think about this. Is someone or something preventing you from realizing your true happiness? Is someone making unlimited withdrawals in your life but is not depositing anything? It might be your own actions or lack thereof. No one else is responsible for your feelings. You get to manage how you respond to things happening in your life.

Do you feel that you were meant to do more in your life? I sure hope so. You may not be able to live the life that you desire because you have learned helplessness. Often, it's *learned generational limitations* that bind our thoughts, abilities, and future. We are raised at times with limits of what we can't do in life. Not only are we raised that way, but we learn it from TV, pop culture, and social media that continue to shape the fabric of our life's attitude. We believe the lies. We acquiesce to living an average life. We need to challenge our current way of thinking and reinvent ourselves for our future and the generations after us.

Life's unfortunate perceived limitations can keep women from reaching their truest potential. Are you getting in your own way of being the woman that you know you want to be? We tend to sometimes want someone or something to save us. Who are you waiting on to save you? Do you realize that it's your mindset that has a strong hold on your ability to understand that you get to choose and decide how to live your life?

Understanding more about who we are and how we show up in the world is driven by our emotional intelligence. This is the number one skill to becoming a Heckuvachic. If you don't find a way to positively transform your mindset and enhance your emotional intelligence, you will continue to live an unfulfilled life because you won't be totally comfortable with who you are or your purpose in life. You need to explore what your emotional triggers are so that you can learn how to best control your emotions. If you can't control your emotions, you won't be able to control your life. If you can't control your life someone or something, does IT for you.

Are you easily bothered by life stressors? You can't let life constantly overwhelm you. Feeling overwhelmed is triggered by your thoughts. If you believe you're overwhelmed, then you will be overwhelmed. Our feelings are controlled by our thoughts, and that is why it's so important to be in tune with our emotions. We experience so many emotions daily, from joy and peace to despair and disappointment.

Emotional intelligence requires us to understand our personal, social, and emotional competence. When we look at personal competence this means that this is the ability to be aware of our own emotions, motives, and mood. We need to be cognizant of how our emotions affect others. We often hear people say, "you better think before reacting," it's so very true. Our thoughts will get us into heated fellowship that tends to become exacerbated by our lack of emotional control. When we examine social competence, this means that we are socially aware of others' feelings and emotions. This requires a degree of showing both empathy and compassion towards others. This is the skill we use to develop and sustain successful relationships, especially if we are good at it. This skill helps us to connect with others.

The way that we apply emotional intelligence in our daily lives is to understand that our emotions drive our choices, decisions, and behaviors. It is our feelings that make us who we are. When people catch you off guard and say something disrespectful to you, then it's up to you to decide how to respond. Before reacting think about their intent and what your end goal is. Do they align? Is it worth a fight? Take the time to become aware of your thoughts. Our thoughts and beliefs triggered by our emotions can often make us feel stuck in life.

When we find ourselves sinking in quicksand in life, this causes us to become stuck. You must take a stand for yourself. You don't have time to be stuck. This happens when we lack clarity on how to put one foot in front of the other. We tend to believe we don't have options. We fail to see the possibilities. Life tests us from time to time, and the goal is to persevere even when we don't know what the outcome will be.

How is your day-to-day life getting in the way of you persevering and knowing your life's purpose? Often, we are so busy with our kids, fur babies, significant others, family, volunteer activities, faith-based activities, and so on. We are so busy, but we are not being productive. Are you making good use of your time? "Woe is not me" must be your theme if you are constantly being unproductive in making the life you want.

Are you pouring into others and not filling your own cup in return? Do your actions reflect your values? Do you feel loved? Do you suffer from self-doubt? Are you questioning everything? How did you let yourself get to the bottom of your own totem pole?

If you are anything like me, you do have moments where you're seeking peace, direction, comfort, serenity, and re-solve. To me, these should be a given in this thing we call life. But unfortunately, we won't experience these things all the time. Living a life of complacency cannot fulfill you long term. My hope is that you are not living a lie. You don't re-quire a cosigner for your life's journey. And guess what? We also don't need to depend on anyone else to live it either.

Every day is a new day. You do have options. What exactly are you going after? Do you have direction in your life? I dare you to have the desire to change your life. I double-dog dare you to resist the desire to live life as it is. Hold yourself to a higher standard. Aren't you bigger than that?

We must be committed to taking our lives back. Give your-self permission to be great. Trust your instincts.

Only you know you. Don't let anyone steal your joy. My hope for you is that you will be able to move your life for-ward. Life's adversities change us. They forever leave an imprint on our thoughts, beliefs, and values. Experiencing life and understanding that if you own your own power, which is emotional intelligence, you will be able to carry out your life's purpose. I want you to say, "Wow, I have messed around and figured out my life's purpose. I know who I want to become."

Let's choose purpose over perfection. We can strive for perfection, but where would that get us? That is how we got here. So many expectations of what life is and what it should be. We don't have to follow anyone's rules. Let me ask you a question. Do you wear white after Labor Day? I bet you don't. Society and the fashion world sold this to you, and you bought it. Does it really matter? It's that simple. We can't allow anyone else to dictate how we should live.

When we know our purpose and can fully walk in our fortitude, we can become more empowered than ever before. I am a living testimony that proves that life can be restored. *You* can be restored!

You may be experiencing learned helplessness. Learned helplessness happens when someone has unwanted situations that occur, and they can change their circumstances but refuse to do so. Are you always the victim? Sometimes we feel this way when we have not quite let go of the things that hold us back. Your emotional baggage could potentially hold you back from moving forward. You are still holding on to life's unfortunate setbacks. You've not done the work necessary to understand the past so that you can write the next new exciting chapter in your life.

You may be confused, hurt, disgruntled, and stuck in a world of confusion and disappointment. It's human to feel this way, but you've got to get to the point of self-reflection, accountability, and perspective. You may feel like the world has done you wrong. You may have had unfortunate circumstances happen in your life, but I am here to tell you that your life has meaning.

You have a purpose. Being a permanent victim is not okay. Woe is *not* me! We must get past these limiting beliefs. Limited perceptions of reality will take you away from what you want. This doesn't mean that you will forever be free of self-doubt. We don't always have to be in survival mode. What is the payoff if you hold on to life's mistakes, regrets, and adversities? Often survival mode kicks in when we feel anxiety and uncertainty.

You must wonder exactly what makes us change our mindsets. It is imperative that you begin to choose *you*. You deserve it, and you have to believe that you are your biggest priority.

Sometimes its fear that prevents us from making the necessary changes we need or should be making in our lives. Our sense of urgency is relative. We move, change, and pivot when we want to.

What if you were able to let it go? "I'm stuck." "I can't." You hear the voice of the past. Your inner self talks too much, don't you think? Your thoughts tell you so many stories, which are called limiting beliefs. "I can't." "I don't have time."

"I'm too busy." She tells you every mistake you've made. She reminds you of your negative thoughts.

All too often, we forget ourselves in the shuffle of our everyday lives. Are you living a life of complacency? That doesn't work for a woman who wants to turn her dreams into plans. Sometimes our failures, or failure to act, are built on the lies we tell ourselves in our minds. Are you having continued thoughts of despair? Trouble can't last always.

When life brings us curveballs, lemons, or the short end of the unlucky stick, we need to leverage these experiences to make us better and stronger. Since we know that these unanticipated challenges are inevitable, we must get to the point where we transform our mindsets to deal with them and tackle them head-on.

For instance, in 2019, I had to use my newfound life skills and strength to help me through a situation that could have impeded my health. I presented to my ob-gyn office for a routine examination. The doctor completed the exam and said, "I'm concerned about your ovaries." She then ordered an X-ray of my ovaries.

I asked her why she was doing this, and she said she wanted to rule out ovarian cancer. Much to my surprise I felt nothing immediately after she said this. I instantly thought, *well, if this is what's happening to me then I will fight my ass off to be here for my girls.*

I had the X-ray done and then I just waited for the results. And I waited. And I waited some more. After two-and-a-half weeks I still hadn't received my results yet. So, I messaged my care team in the patient portal, and simply said, "Do I have cancer or what?"

Yep. I said it . . . I wasn't angry, I just wanted to know the results. I quickly got a response and my provider apologized for the delay and said that my study was benign. I was grateful and relieved. I was able to manage my thoughts, mindset, and my emotions during this process because I knew that my fate was clearly out of my control. I also recognized that I got to choose my own attitude during the wait-and-see time. I could have lashed out at everyone around me. I could have been angry all day, and in my feelings. I could have become very bitter, cold, and distant. But why? What was that going to achieve? Often people take their feelings and emotions out on the people around them. It's not okay.

Your life is worth reshaping. You can make the necessary mind shift in your life. I want you to look in the rearview mirror and say goodbye to the former you. Here's how we make it happen . . .

CHAPTER 2

Becoming a Heckuvachic!

"This woman has fought a thousand battles and is still standing. Has cried a thousand tears and is still smiling. Has been broken, betrayed, abandoned, and rejected. But she still walks proud, laughs loud, lives without fear, loves without doubt. This woman is beautiful. This woman is humble. This woman is you." —Unknown

CHAPTER 2

Becoming a Heckuvachic!

We must be brave in the face of adversity. Therefore, I want to help motivate you in your journey to becoming a Heckuvachic. To become a Heckuvachic you must first make the decision that this is what you want to be. You must make the choice to live life differently. This begins with first being willing to commit to building a growth and resilient mindset.

To grow your mindset, you must start by agreeing that your emotional intelligence must be enhanced. It is my hope that you will gain a deeper emotional connection to who you are as a powerful woman in this life by enhancing your emotional intelligence. When you enhance your emotional intelligence, you can be clear about who you are and how you show up in the world. Your emotions are what's keeping you stuck from living life to the fullest.

If you can manage your emotions, you can manage your life. Life's unfortunate setbacks will occur, but it's how you manage your emotions that truly grows your mindset. Often, we lack the ability to be self-aware of how we respond emotionally to things in our lives.

Who taught you how to deal with life's roadblocks? Where did you learn your womanhood? Of course, our mothers, bonus mothers, aunts, grandmothers, and sisters prepared us for womanhood. I would contend that they did the best they could with what they had and how they were taught. However, in these days and times, it's important that we learn new tools to deal with life head-on.

When life is good, and we are just trucking along, we understand that this is the easy part. When life throws its relentless fury of heartache, disappointment, hurt, and pain at us, we must understand how to withstand and endure these setbacks. We know that life can suck sometimes. So, therefore we need to be cognizant of life tools and characteristics that can help us to become more powerful as a woman.

Becoming a Heckuvachic means that you are inspired, motivated, and energized, even through life's difficult setbacks and disappointments. Let's further define what exactly a Heckuvachic is.

Ladies, a Heckuvachic is:

When you can feel comfortable and secure with exemplifying these attributes in your everyday life then you can become more powerful than you ever thought you could. It is imperative that we as women take back, and never relinquish our power again.

Who or what is undermining your ability to own your power? Be selective about what type of energy you let into your mind, your spirit, or your space. Transforming our mindsets is so very important because we are only going to do what our thinking allows us to believe. We are constantly minimizing our potential for greatness.

It is through our triumphs that we recognize our greatness when we come out on the other side. I look at life's obstacles as challenges to overcome. I think that we as women need to find our sense of resiliency. Resilience is the ability to bounce back in the face of challenges, losses, and adversity. This is the whole premise of what *Becoming a Heckuvachic* is all about. Resiliency allows us to draw on our own personal power to overcome disappointing setbacks that will (not may) come our way.

Life can be peppered with suffering. You may be suffering in silence. You may be in a place where you are searching for you, your dreams, lost hopes, and lost dreams. Don't let your immediate response to life's inconvenience be one of hopelessness. You must make the decision *today* that you are going to overcome the setback by leveraging these becoming a Heckuvachic attributes and showing life who's *boss*.

There are things in life that you can control but there are things in life you can't control. If we can't control something, then why would we focus our energy on it. It's not a good use of our emotions, time, or energy. Focus on what you can control which is your emotions, decisions, choices, and behaviors.

Now that you know you've discovered what becoming a Heckuvachic really means, it's now time to leverage these attributes for your life makeover transformation. I am going to share with you my proprietary Life Makeover Transformation Model that I have designed, developed, and used in my own journey to being unstoppable in my personal and professional life. As you understand more about what it looks like to have a life makeover transformation, then you will be able to further see the future successful version of you.

There are many reasons why women need a life makeover. I needed a life makeover because I had to change. I wasn't happy. I did not like the direction my life was going. Life hit me hard and tore a hole in my hopes, dreams, and spirit. I had no other option. I had to respond to what life presented to me.

Sometimes we feel stuck in life, and we get to a point where we desire to make a change. Being stuck in life is not easy especially when you don't know where to turn. Often, this is because of fear. Fear drives us to be stuck. Fear is the root of most women's inability to move forward in life. The fear of failure and rejection sets in, and we then rest on the fact that we are stuck and that's just how life will be for us.

Maybe you are searching for your purpose in life. Believe it or not, we want to contribute to others, but sometimes we haven't determined how we get there. We know that life is not just about us as an individual. You may be wondering how you could fulfill your calling or determine how best your skills and talents can be shared among others. The problem is that you don't know what that is, and you need to do some inward soul-searching to figure things out.

Lastly, you might be at a breaking point. Either you will continue to suffer in silence, or you must commit to making a change. The problem is that you want to escape the issues that are going on in your life, but you are struggling trying to figure out how to make it happen. You want to make a better life, but you are uncertain of the unknown.

You will be able to experience a life makeover using my five-step Life Makeover Transformation Model. It shows you step by step how to move through your feelings of being stuck in life to becoming the Heckuvachic you're entitled to be. This model shows you the mindset transformation that you must have to finally be able to turn your dreams into plans. Your life makeover starts today.

1 Feel...the Emotion

2 Forgive...Yourself and Others

3 Free your mind...of the things that no longer serve you

4 Find your voice.... to speak your truth

5 Follow your dreams....to become the Heckuvachic you are entitled to be

BECOMING A HECKUVACHIC
Life Makeover
Transformation Model

CHAPTER 3

Feel . . . the Emotion

"You may not control all the events that happen to you,
but you can decide not to be reduced by them."
—Maya Angelou

CHAPTER 3

Feel . . . the Emotion

Before we look ahead, we must look inward. It's now time for us to become one with our mindset and interrupt our current ideals to grow positive mindsets. The transition to a positive mindset involves us focusing on the bright side of life and expecting positive results. Our mindset is a collection of our inner thoughts, attitudes, and beliefs. They initiate our way of thinking, which in turn affects the way we feel. We become broken at times because of our circumstances.

Cry out to get your healing. *Stop* being so strong and cry. Who said crying is a weakness? Where did we learn this? Crying allows you to release the hurt, pain, confusion, and sometimes anger that needs to be dispelled from your body. I would contend that when we hold in our emotions, and we don't express them our behaviors tend to reflect them in a negative way.

There are so many levels of emotional pain. Pain that is gut-wrenching, pain that is sharp and is quickly resolved, or long-lasting pain that has to be dealt with methodically and courageously. You must be vulnerable to deal with un-resolved pain. It can't be masked.

When my late husband passed away, I remember crying for days—actually, months. He passed away in April, and every day, especially holidays, was sheer and utter terror. Mother's Day was so very tough. He and our girls would always make that day very special for me. Then came the very first Father's Day my children would experience without their father. I was determined for them not to have to be home for their Father's Day without him. I surprised them with a trip to Orlando. I was hoping this would help alleviate my children's sad memories of their dad on this holiday. Undoubtedly it helped me too. I just wanted to see them smile and have fun. It was also our first trip without him.

I share this because I need you to understand my thoughts and emotions. I began to feel things I never thought I would in a million years. My emotions were all over the place. I became a recluse. My thoughts were empty. I was empty. My heart was broken. I didn't want to focus. I didn't want to feel. I eventually realized that I needed to get away, so I traveled alone to the Bahamas in July on what would have been our ten-year wedding anniversary.

I stayed at an all-inclusive resort filled with couples. I chose this option so that I wouldn't have to leave the resort for anything. Everything was on-site, and it was very convenient. While there, I remembered feeling so many emotions. I was in uncharted territory. I'm usually in control of my emotions, and I rarely am an emotional woman. I felt scared, lonely, sad, mad, jealous, confused, angry, insignificant, abandoned, exhausted, doomed, and destined for forever loneliness.

After being at the resort for three days, I had an encounter with a couple that had apparently seen me at events, the café, and at different restaurants. Early one afternoon, this joyful couple stepped on the elevator with me from the lobby. The lovely woman said to me, "I've seen you walking around the resort since you've been here." She goes on to ask, "Where is your husband?" I guess she saw my ring finger, and I had on my wedding ring. I immediately was offended that she had the audacity to be intrusive. She asked me a very personal question, but it quickly reminded me that my role as a wife was no longer. I was now a widow. I thought you only became a widow later in life when you were well into your sixties, seventies, or eighties. So, I answered the woman. I simply said, "I'm here alone. My husband died of a terminal illness three months ago, and today would have been our ten-year anniversary." The woman gasped, burst into tears, and collapsed into her husband's arms. She looked at me as though I had offended her, but I recognized that my answer to her question caught her completely off guard and it startled her.

When I exited the elevator and entered my villa, I noticed that I didn't have any emotion after saying what I had to this couple. That was the first time that I didn't feel anything.

At that moment I recognized that I needed to purge my relentless pain. So, I got a beach cabana and lay on the beach for eleven hours. I cried, and I cried. I ate lunch. I put my toes in the sand, and then I lay back down. I cried, and cried, and cried. I ordered a snack. It was so yummy. I sat there staring at the beach around me. I hoped that he, the man I married, would just magically appear out of the water and console me over his own death. I had so much hurt, despair, and pain built up inside of me that I had been carrying for a very long time. I had to be so strong. The release of emotion had a positive impact on my feelings and emotions. After a few more days at the resort, I returned home with a renewed focus and a sense that maybe there was a chance I could endure life.

I thought, *I am a widow, but one day, damn it, I will go from surviving, to thriving, to dominating.* God made me imperfect, but this too will pass. I will be able to enjoy life one day. Maybe not anytime soon, but one day.

Getting to a place where I could try and recover from the agony, disappointment, brokenness, sadness, and grief really pushed me beyond my limits. It was not an easy task. I realized that my thinking had to shift to a more positive outlook on life if I wanted to begin thriving. I had to be open to the possibility that my life could become fulfilling. I encourage you to truly feel your emotions whenever and wherever you want and then let them go and come out swinging.

What emotions are you feeling right now? Sadness? Loneliness? Hurt? Confusion? Misery? Misunderstood? Lost? Anger? Our emotions can be painful, but I declare that if you stick with my Life Makeover Transformation Model, it will give you a renewed mindset, which is the best way to approach a needed life transformation.

To raise your self-awareness, learn, grow, and take the next steps to moving into your purpose in life, you will need to identify the feelings that are holding you back from making the necessary changes in your life. Is it fear? Do you have anxiety? Are you broken? Do you feel lonely? Are you feeling numb? Do you struggle with feelings of being lost?

Having different emotions is okay. It's what makes us human. Many times, because we can't have what we want in life we feel an unusual and unwelcome sense of pain.

We can't deny pain. It will rear its super-ugly head and come to the surface. When it does, I implore you to see it, hear it, process it, and feel it. Think about why it bothers you. What can it do to you? What if this same pain happened to a loved one? Would you want it to destroy them and get in their way of progressing in life? Think about that for a moment. We can't hide from our emotions. They come and just sit on our chests, or we feel it in our gut. Sometimes it feels a little dull, like having a splinter in your pinky finger, and sometimes it feels like a firecracker going off in your belly. There is peace after those tears, girl.

I want you to experience positive things like joy, success, peace of mind, pleasure, recognition, a sense of belonging, and connection, because you have been able to do the work necessary for your growth. Your soul will be free when you are comfortable with how you show up as a woman and your outside beauty matches your beauty within.

CHAPTER 4

Forgive . . . Yourself and Others

"True forgiveness is when you can say,
"Thank you for that experience.""
– Oprah Winfrey

CHAPTER 4

Forgive . . .Yourself and Others

Make peace with your past to solidify your future. Don't let hurt and shame bury you. You're much stronger than that. Be vulnerable to your life's story. We have to go through the process of healing. Healing involves feeling your emotions, and you can't heal without forgiveness. Forgiveness is not about others. It's about you. Yep, *you*! Come to grips with how you process your hurt, pain, anger, rejections, or disappointment. Are there folks you need to apologize to? This breakthrough is for you.

Forgiveness is a powerful word, and it leads to a perspective of reaching beyond yourself to create internal peace. I've had to forgive others who have done me wrong, deceived me, or betrayed my trust. I've had to forgive people who may or may not actually know that their actions played a part in me feeling awful. Your unresolved lack of forgiveness can take a toll on your personality and psyche.

I've also learned to forgive myself. I've not always been the best daughter, sister, wife, mother, teammate, or friend. Clearly none of us are perfect. We make mistakes. In life we sometimes fall short of people's expectations, and many times people let us down. It's a part of life.

Look at your life journey. You have been tested, tried, and challenged throughout your life. These things are a true prerequisite to living the life that you want. For instance, I had to do something difficult in the summer of 2013. This is not the most comfortable life story to share, so please bear with me.

I've had irregular menstruation cycles all my life. In June, my cycle began, and it lasted for four weeks straight. I told myself if it didn't stop in a week, I would go to the doctor. Well, as life got busy being a wife and mother, another week and a half went by. On the morning of August 6, 2013, I woke up to get ready for work. I walked into my closet to pull out my work clothes. Suddenly, I felt a sharp and excruciating pain that was like a bolt of lightning in my chest, belly, and back. The pain was so unbearable that I literally fell to my knees. I crawled to my husband to get help. He picked me up like I was an infant and laid me down on the bed. I called the ob-gyn and made an appointment for later in the day. I then fell asleep because I felt so incredibly tired.

When I awoke, I felt okay to drive myself to the doctor's office. When I arrived, I was so nervous. I thought that maybe I was going through early menopause at the age of thirty-six. When I was called back to the exam room, I explained to the doctor what was happening and then he asked if he could examine me. I agreed, and he began. After what felt like a lifetime, the doctor said, "Ma'am, you are miscarrying."

I replied, "Miscarrying what?"

He said, "You are pregnant, and you're miscarrying a baby." He began to talk, but I didn't hear anything else he said. He stayed there for about ten more minutes as my eyes filled with tears. I was in shock. I did not know I was pregnant. I was alone. This just couldn't be. How can you be pregnant and not know? My doctor was very empathetic and compassionate. He apologized for my loss and then said he needed to see me in a few days to monitor my HCG levels.

The doctor gave me a prescription for antibiotics and said I had to come back in two days. I was incredibly emotional, and I drove home crying and hyperventilating. I walked in the house and went to sleep. I slept for hours. When I awoke, I told my husband what had happened. As I was telling him, my mind and my heart were not in sync. I couldn't believe the words that I was saying.

I would later find out at a follow-up visit that I had been between three to four months pregnant. At the time, I felt a mix of emotions. I was riddled with guilt, shame, and regret. I resented myself for not knowing I was pregnant. My unborn baby didn't have any prenatal care. I wasn't taking prenatal vitamins. I wasn't drinking enough water. I was not taking care of myself. The level of blame that I brought onto myself was palpable. I felt trapped in a place where I was in such pain, but I couldn't seem to get through or over it. Why me? I didn't see my unborn child, and I couldn't get past it. I would see families with newborns and feel sickened as I yearned for my baby. Then I wondered if it was a boy or a girl.

The agony of not knowing there had been a baby inside of me and that I failed to care for it, disgusted me. My husband supported me through this situation. He repeatedly told me that it wasn't my fault. I just couldn't let it go. I beat myself up and felt a sense of embarrassment, shame, and anger. I had feelings of guilt and outrage. How long was I going to let myself stay down? Months went by, I continued to process what had happened, and I began to slowly surface from the fog. I had to be honest with myself. My mindset had to change. I had to come to the obvious conclusion that it would not be in my character to neglect a baby living inside of me. I finally got it. It was at that moment that I realized I didn't know I was pregnant, and I knew that if I had, I would have been a responsible woman and ensured that my unborn baby received proper prenatal care.

I needed to get past the guilt, shame, and resentment that I had toward myself. I forgave myself for having ridiculous thoughts of inadequacy and ignorance. After all, I already had children at that time, and I was and still am a damn good mom. Once I realized I needed to forgive myself, that's just what I did.

As I'm writing this, I am sadly reminded that I lost my unborn baby and my late husband in the same hospital, which ironically was also where I worked.

Forgiving yourself is freeing. I remember as a young child, if someone did something to me that I didn't like, I would tell my mother. She would listen intently, and then I would say it just wasn't fair. Her famous quote was, "Life isn't fair."

It stuck with me. Turns out she was so right. Not everything in life will go your way.

Have you ever been emotionally abandoned or hijacked by someone? This is another instance where we lose ourselves. When you are feeling rejected, marginalized, or devalued, I urge you to take it for what it's worth. If this happens, we don't have to beg anyone to love us, respect us, or treasure us.

I've been rejected in my life. It hurts. But I was able to move past it. If you fail to set healthy boundaries to attract the connection, love, and respect you deserve, then you will continue to suffer. You will continue to wonder why you are not good enough. You'll wonder if there was anything you could have done differently for this person to like you. Nope. It doesn't work that way.

Sometimes we can get lost in love, or what we *think* is love. As women, we sometimes lose ourselves making everyone else around us happy at all costs. The cost can add up, and when we count the costs, our self-identities often get the biggest distribution of the bill. We can no longer do this.

This can happen in your professional life as well. Forgiveness can sometimes suck. You don't want to forgive someone you care nothing about, but again, forgiveness is not about anyone else but you.

Let's face it: we are hard on ourselves. Sometimes we as women are so compassionate and empathetic that it immobilizes us. Our thoughts and feelings are often dismissed because we care so much. It's how we are built. We wonder why life's curveballs throw us for a loop.

Are you taking accountability for your own behavior? A Heckuvachic takes personal accountability and responsibility for her behavior or lack thereof. Projecting your anger and fury onto others is a form of self-hate. How did you get there? Are you in a toxic relationship with your significant other, family member, friend, or coworker? Self-hate can block blessings. Feel your emotions. Express your emotions. Stop holding it in.

You've got to trust your heart. You know that you deserve better in life, and I know that you already know this, but you fail to make the changes necessary to go after the life you deserve.

Failure is impossible if you have the fortitude necessary to put one foot in front of the other. When you change your mindset, you will quickly see that failure is just an opportunity to learn. You are not a screwup. Yes, you've made mistakes. Not only are we human, but we are imperfect. Resentment can often impact our inner spirit, even though we try to mask it. I want you to show up for yourself. I recognize that you have battle wounds. We cannot give what we don't have. Walk in forgiveness.

Forgiveness is one of the keys to a life of clarity. Begin to be honest with yourself and your ability to be open to forgiveness. At times we may not want to forgive, but life can really bless you if you can forgive yourself and others. Other people will disappoint you. They will let you down. No one owes us anything. When you realize this you will gain a better understanding of why it's imperative that you forgive because then and only then will you be able to gain your true internal freedom.

CHAPTER 5

Free Your Mind . . . from the Things That No Longer Serve You

"All the world is full of suffering.
It is also full of overcoming." —Helen Keller

CHAPTER 5

Free Your Mind . . . from the Things That No Longer Serve You

Before you free your mind, you will need to transform your mindset. Your first step is to reframe your thinking. Being an empowered woman means refusing to settle for things that no longer serve you. We cannot afford to limit ourselves. What are you tolerating or coping with in life that's keeping you from being great?

You don't have to compromise your values, morals, and upbringing to make the necessary moves that you need. You need to embrace strong personal boundaries to push yourself to become the Heckuvachic you know you want to be.

Who or what are you consciously or unconsciously allowing to run, dictate, or control your life? This is not healthy or sustainable. Who's ruffling your feathers? Someone who has the victim mentality constantly blames others, including the devil, for situations that occur in the world. Don't give people or the devil so much power or credit.

Freeing my mind is sometimes pervasive. I am constantly thinking and processing things repeatedly. When my husband passed away, I obviously became a single parent. It seemed very unfair. It wasn't that I was co-parenting with an ex-husband. I literally became the only parent to my children.

That was a very new role for me. Although I grew up in a single-parent household and my mom was a great role model, it took me some time to adapt to this new role of mine. I kept overthinking my role as a mom just because I was a single parent. I was very upset that I was made a single parent through no fault of my own.

I was disappointed that my children would also be raised in a single-parent household. I remember not liking that feeling as a child, and now this is what my children would have to experience. My father was a good dad and present in my life, but it's nothing like living and being raised by both parents in the home. It wasn't fair . . . but remember what my single-parent mom said . . . "Life is not fair." It was so challenging to let this new reality become a part of my future.

I also had to come to grips with a tragic situation that occurred in the fall of 2018. I had a speaking engagement at a national conference in Orlando, Florida. My mom and sister kept my children for me. After the conference, I traveled back home. I was so excited to see my children, mom, and sister.

When I awoke the next day, on Thursday, November 15, I didn't know that my knees would buckle during my miscarriage. My mother had two scheduled doctors' appointments that day in Atlanta, GA which is where I live. My mother lives in South Carolina. So, we got the kids off to school and went to the first doctor's appointment. My sister and I noticed that Mom was not her usual jovial and energetic self. She said she felt sick and needed a peppermint to calm down her nausea. This really helped.

After a short while, we went to lunch. She didn't eat much. She began to say she was tired. We told her that she could get rest right after her second doctor's appointment, which was in an hour. We assured her that she could rest after the doctor's appointments while on the drive back to South Carolina.

When we got into the exam room at the afternoon doctor's appointment, the medical assistant checked all her vitals. I recall him checking again. He saw the results and darted out the door to get help. The physician then shared the results of her blood pressure, which was in a dangerously fatal range. He told us to take her to the nearest emergency room immediately.

My sister and I got her in my car. I looked at my mom, and she didn't look good. She was slowly losing her color, and she couldn't open her eyes. She couldn't speak. I began to speed and was going 115 miles per hour all the way with my flashing lights on. It took me all of ten minutes to get to the ER.

Within seven minutes of arriving, we were told that she was suffering a heart attack and she would need to undergo immediate emergency surgery. The healthcare providers began to rip my mother's clothes off to prepare for surgery, and in three more minutes, she was in the operating room.

After the healthcare team rolled her away from the bay, I fell again to my knees in utter shock, dismay, pain, and anger. I looked up and the chaplain was at the door. Did the chaplain know something I didn't know? The chaplain asked if she could help me, and I couldn't focus on the words that came out of her mouth. I immediately thought, *Lord, you took my husband two years ago; please don't take my mom.*

I began to pace incessantly, and my sister and I just held each other and prayed. We were both in shock about what was happening. It didn't make sense. Why, Lord, why? I kept asking the Lord to please show up for my mom. I needed her. My whole family needed her.

Why was this happening? After surgery, my mother spent the next seven days in the ICU. My emotions were all over the place. I needed my mother. She's the strongest woman I know. She survived and was thankfully discharged on Thanksgiving Day.

It would take her a year of hard work and cardiac rehabilitation to recover from this health nightmare, but she did it. I was so very proud of her and grateful. I still questioned my faith and my sanity. So much tragedy in such a small window of time.

As time went on, I realized again that I needed to reframe and change my mindset as I mentally and emotionally healed from this unfortunate incident. I came to the realization that I didn't need to question my faith as I always had when I was fearful in tragic situations.

My savior saved my mom's life, and that's what I had to focus my thoughts on. I had to gain clarity. If my mom wasn't at a doctor's appointment but instead had been home alone, we would have lost her. If the hospital she presented to was not the best in town, we could have lost her. If she left the doctor's appointments and then traveled back to South Carolina chances are again we would have lost her.

Either way, God spared her life. She's here with us and is continuing to do well and her spirits are brighter than they had been in a long time.

The way everything happened that day, my God was right there every step of the way, and this helped me to free my mind of the things that no longer served me. I noticed that my mind became more willing to refuse to take the bait of diminishing my faith. No! Not going to happen. My faith was restored, and my mom had a great recovery journey. She is as active as she ever was. I will be forever grateful for the grace and mercy shown by God in this instance.

Do you ever feel lost? Hesitancy comes from fear, guilt, or shame. Stop being bitter. Bitter women can become so toxic, and at times they spew out their pain onto others.

If you are a bitter woman, there is someone in your life paying the price for that. Folks in the back, did y'all read that?

Bitter women take their aggravation, frustration, depression, anxiety, and anger out on other people. No one I know wants to be subjected to this kind of wrath from a person, whether personally or professionally.

This can be off-putting for those who are unfortunately in the line of fire of your rage and disappointment. Stop blaming others for your unresolved emotional issues caused by life's roadblocks. If you choose to continue this behavior, you may find yourself alone and just angry as hell by yourself.

What aspects of your life do you want to change? Ask yourself if you have meaningful and successful relationships with your significant other, children, family, friends, or coworkers. Has someone you once adored just ghosted you without explanation? Most of the time it's their fault, but sometimes, sis, it can be ours.

Let's work on your spirit. You can't hide in your shadows. I need you to choose the light. Search for the light. You know how bugs are attracted to light when the room is very dark? I need you to seek the light just like bugs. No matter how dark your world is, there is light on the other side. You've got to believe this.

Sometimes what prevents us from having healthy relationships is that we hold on to what could be or think we can fix our partners. We also tend to see life only through our own lens. If something is not going the way we think it should, then we project our disapproval because our way is the only way.

What generational curses are impacting your life today? Often who we were as children and teens shows up in our adulthood. We must take a look at how we grew up. Did you grow up in a generation where kids were to be seen but not heard? I did. Additionally, your opinion was kindly handed to you. Our ancestors passed this on from generation to generation. I know without a doubt that they did the best they could with what they had. I am not knocking the ideology, but it does have flaws.

This train of thought is not healthy or empowering. If we don't practice decision-making when we are younger, then how do we expect children to grow into adults empowered to live their own lives and make decisions? Do our thoughts and feelings not matter as children? This is how we sometimes grow into adults ill-prepared to deal with our emotions effectively, both personally and professionally.

We have self-doubt, and this impacts our self-confidence. We then seek refuge and validation from everyone except ourselves because we were not raised to feel secure in our own self-assurance.

Honor yourself by believing in yourself. You don't need anyone to validate you constantly. It's okay to begin to see yourself as your own hero. You are not a mistake. Your life's journey is not a mistake. All of this was intended for you to make your breakthrough. Think about it.

You have so much to give. In all the roles I have had in my life, I've never put *me* first. It cost me, and it cost me big.

It caused anxiety, depression, and constantly feeling unfulfilled. I didn't even know how I got there.

Is your soul ready for what God has for you? You can be delivered from your pain. Failure happens to all of us. It's how we learn and grow from it that becomes the defining moment in our lives. All of us come from different backgrounds. Some of us had excellent childhoods and some of us, not so much. You don't have to become what you were negatively exposed to.

Don't you sometimes feel like you must be something to so many somebodies? Refuse to compromise who you genuinely are to please your significant other, friends, family, or anyone else. You don't have to have all the answers. Know when to say *no*. You matter!

Have you made sacrifices of time, money, or energy for things that do you no good?

Are you so strong that you think you are superhuman? Well, you are, but that doesn't mean that you must be strong twenty-four seven. If you look back at the attributes of a Heckuvachic, you will notice that it says to be strong at times. If we focused our energy on being strong all the time, our mental and physical health could suffer. When we are always strong, we tend to take on stress in our lives that soon can take us under. Continued stress can actually kill you.

There will be times when you need to be vulnerable. Asking for help is not a sign of weakness. It means that you are resourceful. It's a sign of security, integrity, and, most of all, strength. You are bigger than your prior, current, and future circumstances. What work do you need to do to find peace within yourself?

Are people in your life paying for your unresolved issues, trauma, drama, and tragedies? Chances are you have done this or are doing this. Is this fair? Why are you doing this? Would you like it if these things were done to you? Are your significant other, children, family members, coworkers, or boss paying for the pain you carry?

You get to be selective in your relationships, whether they are family, romantic, working, or community relationships. Trust your intuition. We as women were born with power. Stop comparing yourself to others. You are courageous. You are gorgeous. You've come so far.

What kind of energy are you bringing? Insecurity has no place in your life. Get back up when you fall. We cannot diminish ourselves for others, and we are certainly not dimming our light for someone else's comfort. This goes for whoever in your life is taking you for granted and doesn't appreciate who you are and your place as the queen you are.

All too often we beg for love. We beg for relationships. It is our own insecurities and self-doubt that prevent us from seeing the bright, shiny, candy-coated red flags of a new romantic partner. Your vulnerability, lack of awareness, and discontent with life can cause you to become prey to predators. That's why clarity is so very important. It opens our eyes to what we couldn't see before.

We are so committed to the thought of what could be that we don't focus on the now in someone's behavior toward us. We now know that when someone shows their true colors, we need to take heed and believe them. Sometimes men desire their wives as well as their side girlfriends. How is that fair to you? Once we know better, we must always do better.

When a romantic partner wants you, you will know. You are not someone's second best. If a person doesn't want you, thank them and keep it moving. *You don't have to beg for love, a proposal, or a marriage.*

We have to put ourselves first. This is your first line of defense if you don't know anything else. Ladies, we must listen to our guts and instincts, so we don't have to pay the ultimate price, which is our womanhood. To transform your mindset, you must start with who you are as a woman, and this involves understanding your emotional intelligence so that your being can be whole. When we are not whole, we are only a fraction of ourselves. We then give the other part to whoever is available.

We must remove self-doubt from our mindsets. Most of the time when we want more out of life, we let these little things stop us in our tracks. Mediocrity doesn't work for me. Stop settling in your romantic, career, or family relationships.

You must find the motivation to leave what is secure and comfortable to make favorable life changes. Let's talk about boundaries. As women, we especially must set boundaries. Yes, we are superwomen, and we have the S on our chests to prove it. However, when you are too busy being superwoman, your life becomes robotic. You're not able to be in the moment to enjoy life's precious moments. Setting boundaries for yourself and those around you is very important. It also means that you will need to stand up for yourself. It's very challenging to set boundaries when you have been a certain way for a long time.

What boundaries have you not enforced? We need to set personal boundaries with those we meet. We need to have personal, emotional, financial, sexual, spiritual, and physical boundaries. Think of it this way. Say no when you want to say no! No is a two-letter word and a whole sentence. Develop consequences for anyone who crosses your boundaries. Describe what you want instead.

You will also need to create healthy boundaries to attract the love and respect you deserve and to maintain your relationship with your significant other.

Do you always feel exhausted? What are you really saying to yourself? You are being inundated because of the way you are thinking and processing your inner thoughts. At times, it's self-imposed. Why? Because you've answered yes to all the above and forgot to set boundaries. Boundaries are needed in our relationships with family, friends, and coworkers.

When you say no, some folks may not like it and they may react to it. It's all fun and games until you let people know that you can't be controlled, manipulated, or marginalized anymore. When you finally stand up for yourself, you will quickly notice that not everyone will be happy about it. Some people will not like it all, and that's okay. Life is too short to live on anyone else's terms, expectations, or rules of engagement. They will have to grieve the old you, but they will survive.

Self-esteem issues can keep you from reaching your full potential. It can keep you stuck, like you're sinking in quicksand. You will no longer be mistreated by emotional abuse or violence. The next time someone upsets you by no fault of your own, simply say, "I do not give you permission to ruin my day." You can thank me later.

Have you gone through a terrible breakup or divorce? Instead of seeing it as a horrible experience, maybe take a moment to say, "Wow, I have been delivered from something that didn't make me happy or fulfilled." You must refuse to limit yourself. Life is not about settling for anything and everything. You deserve exactly what you want.

Wouldn't you agree? Settling is for people who don't want or expect more. You can't do that anymore. It's against your new role of choosing yourself and your own life's destiny. Who in your circle is not on your team? Who's taking your energy and dragging your spirit? Get in the habit of not co-signing on bullshit. Take account of your supporters and your haters. I pray for my haters. Haters come in all hates and sizes.

Woulda, Shoulda, Coulda . . . How long will you dwell in the past? Growth happens during our discontent, tests, challenges, tragedies, trials, and tribulations. You do not have to be a product of your environment. You do not need the additions or subtractions. Where you came from does not dictate where you are destined to be.

What do you believe? Do you believe that your life can change? What do you know to be true about what is possible in your life? I know that I am more than grateful to be where I am in life currently. I am very aware that because of my upbringing and where I come from that I could have become a statistic in society. I realize that the God I serve had his hands on me. I have discovered that it was my spiritual faith, which I learned from my Grandmother Sugarchild, my mom, and my dad and that God truly directed my path.

I am indebted to the great mentors that I have had in my life. I am so appreciative of the many people that have poured positivity and encouraging words into my life so that I could become the woman that I am today.

Freeing your mind and letting go of your past emotional distractions and baggage can give you the necessary courage that you need to release yourself from mental bondage and defeat. Imagine your life without letting every little thing wreck your nerves.

CHAPTER 6

Find Your Voice . . . to Speak Your Truth

"'The tongue has the power of life and death.'
The stakes are high. Your words can either speak life,
or your words can speak death. Our tongues can build others
up, or they can tear them down."
—Proverbs 18:21

CHAPTER 6

Find Your Voice . . .
to Speak Your Truth

What is your truth? The truth isn't always easy, pretty, or desired. Are you living a lie? Let your truth help heal you. Are you or do you know someone who is glammed up on the outside and a hot mess on the inside? If so, this person is living a lie, and not living her authentic self in her circles. Do you know who you are without someone else telling you who you are? What's keeping you from being the woman you know you are?

You need to take back your power. Stop faking it until you make it. Be your authentic self. If you don't know how to do something, figure it out! It's okay not to know something, but you need to do what you need to do to acquire the skill, knowledge, or capability that you are seeking. There is no need to subject yourself to being a victim of imposter syndrome. I want to challenge you to reach your highest potential. If something doesn't come naturally to you, then learn it. Let's explore this.

In high school, I was a social butterfly, and I really blossomed. I played the viola in the orchestra, and varsity basketball, and I was captain of the bowling team. I did moderately well in my academics. I was senior class president, president of the SECME (Science, Engineering, Communication, Mathematics Enhancement) club, president of the SADD (Students Against Driving Drunk) club, and president of the Interact club. I was also voted Best All-Round in my senior year and inducted into the senior hall of fame. I excelled in social settings.

In my academic life, I wasn't the best of the best, but I made the honor roll a few times. I didn't really apply myself, and my academics weren't very important to me or a significant priority. I wasn't totally confident in my scholastics, and I had self-doubt. I graduated with a decent GPA, but not one that made me eligible for any scholarships, that's for sure.

I then attended college in the fall. In my first semester I encountered a rude awakening. Not only did I have to adjust to living and being responsible on my own, but I also immediately realized that I was not interested in social involvement anymore. I didn't really do a lot of partying at all. I wasn't engaged with academics either. I felt somewhat unprepared for college-level rigor in my studies, and my first semester grades proved it. Two Ds. What in the world? I had to clutch my own pearls.

Letters I had never seen on any report card. I was devastated and embarrassed that I wasn't doing so well. I went home for the holiday break to tend to my academic disaster. My self-confidence was in the toilet, and I lacked the motivation to do better. I didn't feel competent. I thought maybe I wasn't cut out for college. I wasn't smart enough. I've always been taught that education is the key to my future.

I pondered what would happen to me if I didn't get my education, and what kind of life would I end up having. I wasn't sure if I wanted to go back to school for the next semester. I was so disappointed in myself.

I licked my wounds and went back for the second semester. I remember during the second week I met a friend, Pam. She and I developed a relationship because we shared the same major. One evening when we had our first study group, I learned more about her. I realized that I had never seen her around campus. As we were getting to know each other, she shared with me that she had a young child and was married. I was rather floored by this because I wondered how she was able to be in school and make such excellent grades. I was so impressed. I shared with her my self-doubts about academics. She told me that I could do it and that I just needed to apply myself. I began to internalize what she said when I got home that evening. She was married, had a young child, and was still making excellent grades. I was alone. I didn't have any responsibility but to take care of myself. I had a life-changing mindset transformation that same night.

I said to myself, *"If she can make excellent grades and have to go home and care for her child, run a household, and go to college, there is no excuse for me."* If she could do it, then I needed to get my booty in gear and step up to the plan. I began meeting with all my professors to let them know that

I was serious about my grades and wanted any insight they may have that would help me excel in their classes.

I started learning how to study. I checked out books in the library to learn how to make proper outlines and take effective notes while in college. I became a more focused student in my classes. I became a professional color-coding queen with my notes. My notes had to be pretty. They had to be eye-catching to get my attention. I would review my notes and read assigned chapters in preparation for each school day. If I didn't know how to do something, I would find people who did, and I would learn as much as I could from them. I reserved a study room in the library for about four hours every day. That semester I really applied myself, and I learned what it meant to study successfully. Before long, I brought home my report card. I gave it to my mom and ran up to my room. She began to scream. I wondered what in the world she was screaming about—my grades were clearly a lot better than last time. Then she mumbled something about me making the dean's list. I was like, "Lady, what is that?" She began to laugh as I stood there as serious as ever. She said, "You made the dean's list. It's the honor roll in college." *Hm. You don't say, huh.* In my head, I began to scream. I couldn't let on to her, though. She began to call her friends, especially her church friends, to brag.

I waltzed back upstairs and began to cry tears of joy. I did it. I made myself proud, and it looked like I made her proud too. Wow, that's how that works. Now it's on. Yes! I went on to make the dean's list four times in my college career, and

I was listed in *The National Dean's List*. Since then, I have earned my graduate degree and five certifications.

See, I had to understand my truth. My truth was that I was a subpar student who had the propensity to be a great student. I was overcome with self-doubt. Once I did the work to become an achiever, I continued to believe that I could, and no one or nothing could stop me but me. I became my authentic self, and I was able to speak my truth.

Living your authentic self is all about embodying and agreeing with who you are and what you do. We must let go of expectations other people have placed on us. Your life can feel stagnant if you are so focused on what others think of you because then your life is not your own. I need you to refuse to let others impose their expectations on you. You are more than capable of being the CEO of your life.

I will not allow myself to be emotionally hijacked by anyone. Explore who you are as a woman. Who taught you how to be a woman? How'd that training go? What did you realize about yourself when you became a woman? Our truths can often be uncomfortable. Well, you need to feel that. Understand that the person you are today is doing the best she can, but now she is speaking her truth.

No more talking down to yourself and putting yourself down for the mistakes you have made. It happened, girl. Understand that the hurt you felt is okay. Don't be sour because someone hurt you. Yes, they may have obliterated your heart, but don't you think it's time to relinquish their power over you? There comes a time when you must accept the past so that you can stand in your truth.

Do you know your purpose? What are you seeking? A career or job change? Are you stuck in a job you hate? Tired of the mundane? Are you seeking financial freedom?

Learn a new skill. Do research. Who cares what people think of you? Do they pay your bills? I'm guessing not. So, take back your power and own your ignorance. Don't fake it till you make it. Be your authentic self. If you don't know how to do something, *figure it out!*

How do you rank yourself on your list of priorities? It's okay to be selfish at times. I didn't learn that until later in life. I thought that being selfish was frowned upon as I learned about values and societal expectations.

Being selfish is a form of self-care that is rarely discussed. Yes, as I have mentioned before, you get to put yourself first sometimes. It's okay. It's not taboo. Explore what makes you, *you!* This is very important as it allows you to put a spotlight on yourself.

There is nothing wrong with that. If you don't have a sense of self, then it's very difficult to choose yourself. I challenge you to choose you. Incorporate this in your everyday life, but don't forget to balance it with the needs of your everyday life.

I've learned that when people perceive me and my personality, I'm often told that I am always positive, inspiring, motivational, and energetic.

I had a coworker ask me, "Do you ever have a bad day?"

I said, "Yes, I do have bad days."

She said, "I bet you go home and beat your kids." The comment was comical to me. I have a great sense of humor, so I really was not offended. I get to choose my own attitude, and so do you.

If I'm frustrated about something at work, who cares? That's my thinking. If someone has upset me, do I need to let the world know that I am upset? I don't need to take my frustration or anger out on others. That doesn't mean that I'm not being my authentic self. I most certainly am, but my emotional intelligence allows me to adapt and respond so that I own my power.

When you don't deal with your own emotions proactively your emotions can project intentionally or unintentionally onto others.

For example, we feel that we must become so defensive with people we encounter if they negatively trigger us. You don't have to match your energy with someone else's energy if they are being insensitive or disrespectful.

You can stand your ground with the elegance and choice of your words. This helps to relieve the stress and negative energy that can consume your body. You get to protect your energy, peace, and vitality. In our pursuit of true happiness, we must recognize that stress can be a danger to our overall physical and mental health. By reducing your levels of stress, you can have a clearer head to make life decisions and choices that need to be made. You can improve your blood pressure, have a stronger immune system, sleep better, and reduce tension headaches. That's why it's imperative to own your own power to improve your overall health. Be appreciative of where you are in your life and decide to live it differently. If you are speaking and walking in your truth, then you, my friend, are controlling your own destiny.

What have you done lately to better your circumstances? You must take back any power over your life that you have lost. Once you do that, you will be able to understand and value your power. You will refuse to settle for anything less than the best.

Do you value yourself enough to not settle on a significant other, the car you want, the business you want to open, the school you want your kids to attend, the job you choose, or the house you want? In life we must go after what we want. Sometimes life requires us to compromise. There is a difference between compromising and settling. When you settle in life you accept the fact that you don't have what it is you truly want. Do you want to live a life of settling? Settling causes us to regret our decisions and we tend to continue to be unfulfilled because of these choices.

You've got to embody excellence. You need to demand it. You deserve it. Ladies, you must believe this. You are worth it. Live for yourself.

How many times have you started something and didn't finish it? Can you please take responsibility for that?

Conversely, as women, we sometimes put on airs to appear stronger than we are. There are times when we are not strong in this thing, we call life. Once you learn this, it will give you *life*!!!!!

CHAPTER 7

Follow Your Dreams . . . to Become the Heckuvachic You're Entitled to Be

"The great courageous act that we must all do,
is to have the courage to step out of our history and past
so that we can live our dreams."
–Oprah Winfrey

CHAPTER 7

Follow Your Dreams . . .
to Become the Heckuvachic
You are Entitled to Be

I want you to be willing and committed to making the necessary changes in your life to follow your dreams. Your dreams matter! If you are not happy and fulfilled in your life, I encourage you to make the decision to live life differently. You need to define what your dreams are. I often say the old cliché of dream big, but now I say dream big, then dream bigger than that. You will need to examine all facets of your life to determine exactly where the gaps are in your life. What do you value? What do you want? What do you feel you don't have?

Refocus your present life for greater fulfillment. You get to define what that means. Fulfillment could mean joy, success, peace of mind, happiness, a sense of belonging, pleasure, recognition, improved relationships, or enhanced connections. You are the fearless woman who must define this. By visualizing and experiencing our desired future, we gain a sense of clarity.

It takes motivation and inspiration to overcome the obstacles that occur in our lives. It's up to us to change our mindsets to fulfill life's promise. We all face adversities in life. We either succumb to the devastation of it, or we choose to survive it, and it becomes a defining moment in our lives that makes us stronger than ever before. Don't give up. Push through. Be bold in the face of adversity.

You can change your life forever by choosing yourself first. It's all about putting the oxygen mask on first. This means that we must prioritize our life and put ourselves first in line.

Unfortunately, this is not easy for us to do as women. In a sense, being a powerful woman means that it's okay to be selfish. As children we were taught that being selfish is bad. The truth is that we need to be selfish. We must understand that we have to prioritize our lives and put ourselves first so that we can be our best selves for our family and friends.

If you want to become your ideal self, it will require you to begin identifying ways to fill your own cup. This means that you again find what makes you happy. What gives you positive energy? What gives you joy? What can you do to experience small wins that give you a sense of accomplishment? What do you really want to be in your life at this very moment that you are not?

Conversely, you will also need to identify what's not filling your cup. Who or what is distracting you from going after your dreams? Do you have accountability partners who serve as your cheerleaders? Do you have folks in your life who don't support your dreams and desires? You'll need to make the necessary decisions to set your boundaries accordingly. If you desire to move forward in your life, you must make changes. Guess what? You've known that you needed to make some changes, you just need to focus on the Becoming a Heckuvachic attributes so that you have the ideal mindset to proceed with life transformation.

We were raised to be these strong women who become *everything for* and *to everyone* around us. This thinking set us up for failure. We then live our lives believing this lie. This is how we lose our womanhood and our souls because we are too busy caring for and being there for everyone.

Then we get frustrated and overwhelmed. We blame everyone else for our dissatisfaction and exhaustion in life when we caused it ourselves. We don't really want to take personal responsibility or accountability for this dysfunction because we don't want to admit that we did it to ourselves. We then become furious when we fail to carve out *me time* in our everyday hectic life.

No longer are we waiting for permission to take *me time*. We can't wait for others to give it to us. We cannot be willing to settle on not being able to take me time. I believe that this should be some sort of constitutional right for women. I believe that women are the nucleus of this world, our communities, and our families. Women are the backbone of everything we do in life. In an effort to get to our definition of happy we have to recognize our excellence and value that we bring.

Do you know that it's okay to be happy? It's important to recognize that it's possible to be happy in both your personal and professional life. As I was going through the earlier years of my grief process, I never in my wildest dreams believed I could be happy. I didn't even have the energy, or the desire to even want to dream about being happy in life. I couldn't even fathom a life where I was internally happy.

When I chose to change my mindset to begin going after the life I wanted, I began to dream of things I never thought would be possible for me. I put together a plan to go after my dreams. My dreams were very minimal, but it finally felt great to have dreams. As I began to work on attaining my career, financial, and spiritual goals I began to see what was possible in life.

Your self-doubt can prevent you from reaching your life's full potential. I started to grow confidence in myself and begin to live my life differently with a clearer sense of self. I began to live life with purpose. You are in charge of your life. Once you attain your breakthrough and get clarity on what you really want in life, your dreams become possible.

Not everyone will appreciate your growth and your journey to becoming a Heckuvachic. Becoming a Heckuvachic is not a seamless journey. There will be those who will admire you but express their thoughts in a very unsupportive way. Once you begin to actively become consistent with setting healthy boundaries, saying no when you mean no, and prioritizing your life over others it will not be easy for those around you. They will begin to see a different you. They will notice how you respond to life's positive and difficult moments. Not everyone will be happy for you. Jealousy and envy will rear their ugly heads.

You may have some false starts. You will try, and you may fail. Please know that you can succeed! Continue to put yourself first.

Self-care is key. Self-care is a must for us. You are worthy of self-care. Let's make joy accessible in your life. Refuse to go back to being the same woman you were before you began to read this book.

You will not go backward. Pledge to change the trajectory of your life's journey. What are your strengths? What do you want to grow in? Figure out what achievements you want to go after. Step out of your comfort zone. We tend to grow when we are most uncomfortable.

Let your light shine. I see you. No longer will you gravitate toward the curveballs of life.

One of the epiphanies that you will have as you move into becoming a Heckuvachic is that you will need to decide to get out of your own way. You are destined for greatness. Own your power. Own your strength. Own your courage.

I hope you realize that it's not so bad to live a beautiful life. Forget fear. Fear can destroy and confuse you. Fear can produce self-imposed limits on your life. You can realize your dreams.

Your life means that you were placed here for a purpose. Don't you want to be that woman you most admire?

Become that better you . . .*it's time*!

CHAPTER 8

Turning Your Dreams into Plans!

"The size of your dreams must always exceed
your current capacity to achieve them.
If your dreams do not scare you, they are not big enough."
—Ellen Johnson Sirleaf

CHAPTER 8

Turning Your Dreams into Plans!

Now that you have become a Heckuvachic, it's time to manifest your dreams toward a more fulfilling life. We now must develop our action plans to lay the groundwork for focusing in on our dreams. Live with both intention and purpose.

If you struggle with self-doubt, insecurity, lack of confidence, or direction, your mind won't be able to dream the way you need it to. Make a conscious decision to get rid of the things that no longer serve you. If you don't dream big for yourself, who will do it for you?

I love it when a plan comes together. You survived. Repeat after me: **"I will not have anxiety, insecurity, or fear concerning my life's success."** I want you to step into who you are as a *powerful* woman.

What are your values and goals? You've taken this journey to become a Heckuvachic. I want you to understand that your life's purpose will anchor your thoughts. You are destined for greatness, and with that comes abundance.

Identify your dreams. Decide now that you will experience a life makeover. To attain this, you will need to consider what your short-term and long-term dreams are. Create logical action steps. Invest in you. You will need to make some type of commitment to learn and grow. It's important you choose you, and advance in your life.

Devise a plan to celebrate your wins. Let's take this a step further. When your child, pet, significant other, or a loved one overcomes and has an achievement, what do you do? You celebrate them. Remember to celebrate yourself. You deserve it. As you gain momentum your confidence will continue to grow, and when you see results, you will be more energized to stay the course.

What are your must-haves in life? What kind of lifestyle do you want? What is giving you fulfillment? By envisioning and manifesting our desired future, we often gain the motivation needed to overcome life's obstacles. Now you are empowered and can stand in your truth because you have a better idea of how your emotional intelligence controls your fortitude. We must do life differently.

You must determine your purpose in life. Why exactly are you here? What are you passionate about? To map this out, I encourage you to craft your vision boards. A vision board is a graphical representation of your wishes, goals, and dreams. The objective of having a vision board is to provide you with inspiration and motivation toward achieving what you set out to do in your life. This process allows you to visually see your dreams. The exercise allows you to see where you're going in life.

I want you to *visualize* your dreams.

I want you to *manifest* your dreams.

I want you to *energize* your dreams.

I want you to *upgrade* your dreams.

I want you to *live out* your dreams.

This is what it takes to dream big! Believe in your dreams. You will begin to see your dreams manifest, including those dreams you thought you were unworthy of. When you commit to making a life makeover with your newfound mindset, you will notice that you will begin to shift your thinking daily.

In turn, you will inevitably realize your pursuit of *Becoming a Heckuvachic*!

CONCLUSION:

Let Your Self-Discovery Be Your Life's Breakthrough

"Embrace each challenge in your life
as an opportunity for self-transformation."
—Bernie S. Siegel

CONCLUSION:

Let Your Self-Discovery
Be Your Life Makeover

My self-discovery and life breakthrough have allowed me to experience a life makeover that has changed the path of my life forever. Because I was able to do my work and really go through my own life makeover transformation process, I have been able to realize so many of my dreams and now I am on my fourth vision board. Every single facet of my life has greatly and significantly improved, and I am so grateful for it.

I was able to rebuild my relationship with God and my spiritual well-being saw a tremendous improvement from where I was when I was riddled with grief, feeling stuck, and living my life on autopilot. My girls are blossoming and are extremely intelligent and successful in their academic studies and their social lives. I got married to a wonderful and loving man. He's an awesome father figure in my daughters' lives. Ironically, he has the same initials as my late husband.

I was able to acquire my dream job at a very prestigious and internationally known healthcare organization where I am making a great impact on the lives of both teammates and patients. I love my friends and my social interactions that bring me great joy. I am a businesswoman with my own coaching and consulting practice. I am now a published author.

Because of my life makeover, I have gone from surviving, to thriving, to dominating. I'd love the opportunity to help you do the same. "Put me in, Coach!" I sure will. I enjoy empowering women to overcome life's disappointing setbacks so that they can *Become the Heckuvachics* they're entitled to be.

I became a coach to fulfill my life's purpose to help inspire, motivate, and energize others to transform their current lives into their dream lives. My secret sauce is that I have developed my Life Makeover Transformation Model, which is designed to help women transform their mindsets to become a Heckuvachic.

I invite you to work with me. What do you want to be, do, or have? Let's go on a journey of self-discovery so that we can put you on the path of becoming a Heckuvachic. I want to add value to your life and help transform your mindset so that you can be unstoppable in your personal and professional life.

Let me help you become the best version of yourself so that you can be fulfilled in your life and not stifled because of your limiting beliefs and lack of emotional intelligence. Let's connect so that we can see this breakthrough in your life unfold. Together we can make the impossible possible for you.

Is your soul ready for the changes *you* need in your life? If I expect it for you, then you must *demand* it for yourself. Let's commit together to taking your power back.

Let's turn your *can'ts* into *can*s. Life can be that simple. We can work together to clear the noise in your life so that we can see your future. A better you, a better mindset, and a better life starts with me today. I want you to slay! Slay again! Slay once more!

Let's connect. Follow me on all social media @ksaismycoach. Go to my website to immediately download your FREE copy of my Becoming a Heckuvachic worksheet and journal. www.ksaismycoach.com.

ACKNOWLEDGMENTS

Thank you, Chris, for being my biggest fan, confidant, accountability partner, and cheerleader. To my daughters, thank you for saving my life, being the best daughters ever, and for loving me unconditionally. To my amazing parents, thank you for giving me life and building me into the woman I am today. To my sister, Jessica, who always believed in me and has relentlessly, without fail, encouraged me to go after my dreams, thank you!

NOTES

Angelou, Maya. "You may not control all the events that happen to you, but you can decide not to be reduced by them." Accessed 16 February 2022, Published 2008 https://www.goodreads.com/quotes/425908-you-may-not-control-all-the-events-that-happen-to

Milne, A. A.—Character-Christopher Robin. Winnie the Pooh. "Who said you are braver than you believe stronger than you seem and smarter than you think?" Accessed 15 March 2022, Published 1 April 2020 https://www.sluiceartfair.com/2020/students-help-blog/who-said-your-braver-than-you-believe-stronger-than-you-seem-and-smarter-than-you-think/

Keller, Hellen. "The Open Door," Accessed 15 March 2022, Published 1957 https://www.azquotes.com/author/7843-Helen_Keller/tag/suffering

Provers 18:21. 'The tongue has the power of life and death.' The stakes are high. Your words can either speak life, or your words can speak death. Our tongues can build others up, or they can tear them down." Accessed 19 January 2022. https://stgenparish.org/biblical-reading/what-does-the-bible-say-about-speaking-life-and-death.html

Siegel, Bernie S. "Embrace each challenge in your life as an opportunity for self-transformation." Accessed 2 January 2022, Published 3 June 2021 https://quotepark.com/quotes/1287921-bernie-s-siegel-embrace-each-challenge-in-your-life-as-an-opportun/

Sirleaf, Ellen Johnson. "The size of your dreams must always exceed your current capacity to achieve them. If your dreams do not scare you, they are not big enough." Accessed 15 March 2022, https://www.harvardmagazine.com/2011/05/ellen-johnson-sirleaf-commencement-speech

Unknown. "Not all storms come to disrupt your life, some come to clear your path." Accessed 13 March 2022, https://www.quotespedia.org/authors/a/anonymous/not-all-storms-come-to-disrupt-your-life-some-come-to-clear-your-path-anonymous/

Unknown. "This woman has fought a thousand battles and is still standing. Has cried a thousand tears and is still smiling. Has been broken, betrayed, abandoned, and rejected. But she still walks proud, laughs loud, lives without fear, loves without doubt. This woman is beautiful. This woman is humble. This woman is you." Accessed 13 March 2022, https://tinybuddha.com/wisdom-quotes/i-have-fought-a-thousand-battles-but-i-am-still-standing/

Winfrey, Oprah. "The great courageous act that we must all do, is to have the courage to step out of our history and past so that we can live our dreams." Accessed 11 January 2022, https://www.coolnsmart.com/quote-the-great-courageous-act-that-we-must-24375/

Winfrey, Oprah. 25 Forgiveness Quotes to Help You Let Go of the Past. "True forgiveness is when you can say, Thank you for that experience." Accessed 11 January 2022, Published 11 August 2021 https://www.oprahdaily.com/life/relationships-love/g29995262/ forgiveness-quotes/

Reflections

Reflections

Reflections

Reflections

Reflections

Reflections

Reflections

Reflections

Reflections

Reflections

Reflections

Reflections

Reflections

Reflections

Reflections

Reflections

Reflections

Reflections

Reflections

Reflections

Made in the USA
Columbia, SC
15 July 2022

63489032R00074